Meditation

For Beginners

Monique Joiner Siedlak

OSHUN
PUBLICATIONS

Printed in the United States of America

Second Edition 2018

ISBN-13: 978-1-948834-23-0

ISBN-10: 1-948834-23-5

Published By:

Oshun Publications, LLC

www.oshunpublications.com

Disclaimer

All the material contained in this book is provided for educational and informational purposes only. No responsibility can be taken for any results or outcomes resulting from the use of this material. While every attempt has been made to provide information that is both accurate and effective, the author does not assume any responsibility for the accuracy or use/misuse of this information.

Cover design by Monique Joiner Siedlak

Cover image by Pixabay.com

Logo design by Monique Joiner Siedlak

Logo image by Pixabay.com

Other Books in the Series

Creative Visualization

Astral Projection for Beginners

Reiki for Beginners

A Great Offer!

Want to learn about African Magic, Wicca, or even Reiki while cleaning your home, exercising, or driving to work? I know it's tough these days to simply find the time to relax and curl up with a good book. This is why I'm delighted to share that I have books available in audiobook format.

Best of all, you can get the audiobook version of this book or any other book by me for free as part of a 30-day Audible trial.

Members get free audiobooks every month and exclusive discounts. It's an excellent way to explore and determine if audiobook learning works for you.

If you're not satisfied, you can cancel anytime within the trial period. You won't be charged, and you can still keep your book. To choose your free audiobook, visit:

www.mojosiedlak.com/free-audiobooks

Table of Contents

Introduction

Nowadays, meditation is a topic that can escalate a great deal of confusion. It is often perceived as a type of hippie fad or new age craze. Eastern civilizations, however, have known about the knowledge and the power of meditation for centuries and have been using it to influence their minds and develop awareness.

Joining your body, mind and spirit will provide limitless benefits to your overall health. Meditation is a simple, but life-transforming skill that can help you to relax, enhance understanding about yourself and develop your inherent potential. You are so much more.

With the growing acceptance of meditation, it's incredible to see that simple lessons are often disregarded. The first being that you already know how to meditate.

So, do you want to learn how to meditate? Don't know where to start? This book will help take the mystery out of meditation for beginners. Let's begin.

Chapter One
Why the Misunderstanding?

The main reason for the confusion is because there are several forms of meditation. With each form comes a different technique. This makes meditation for the beginner even more confusing because most don't realize that each form of meditation has to some extent, a different purpose. But it turns out that meditation for beginners really don't have to be complicated.

If you're just learning how to meditate, then it's best to just pick one form of meditation. Prepare to learn it. Practice it persistently. This will make it easier for beginners. If you start jumping from one form to another, you're not going to make any progress. And if you don't see any benefit from your efforts, then you'll give up very quickly.

Some believe that you have to have the skill to achieve total inner silence when you meditate. If the presence of any thought intrudes, then it means that you are doing it wrong.

2/ MEDITATION FOR BEGINNERS

The crucial objective of meditation is to reach total mental silence. The only thing is that when you are just starting out, the need for lessening your mental activity should be in the forefront. Once you can reduce your mental activity by even twenty five percent, you'll begin to feel more relaxed. With that, less stress.

The most important key thing to remember throughout the initial steps of your understanding with meditation is that meditation isn't something you can determine in expressions of success and/or failure. Meditation is a way through your consciousness, and it's something that you can complete with sitting with the purpose of quieting your mind. Your ability to achieve this silence through meditation will certainly improve and deepen over time, but you should never feel as though you are failing just because thoughts arise.

So don't criticize yourself severely if you find your mind wandering as you meditate. Mental wanderings are quite normal. Sometimes, even the most proficient will become lost in a few mental wanderings.

Remember, before you go any further; understand that perfection is not expected when you begin. There are several methods. Pick one. Stick with it. All of this will save you from the aggravation of stressing out and giving up. Take it at your leisure.

Chapter Two
What Is Meditation?

So, specifically what is meditation? Meditation is a process that keeps within the yoga system that is designed to show the intertwining of all living things. Meditation may involve establishing a responsive circumstance for the purpose of studying that state or nurturing a distinct mental response to numerous events, such as empathy. This central harmony is signified as Advaita which means non-dual. Meditation is the actual process of this coming together.

In the Hindu philosophy, meditation is described specifically as a state of perfect consciousness. It is the seventh stage of the yogic path and follows the art of concentration, also known as Dharana. Dhyana in turn go before Samadhi, the state of final liberation or illumination, the final step in Patanjali's eight-limbed system. These three limbs are intricately linked and mutually described as Samyama, the inner practice, or indirect discipline, of the yogic path.

4/ MEDITATION FOR BEGINNERS

Meditation has been used for thousands of years. Meditation initially was meant to further deepen consciousness of the spiritual and mystical influences of life. Nowadays, meditation is commonly used for relaxation as well as stress reduction.

Meditation is thought to be a type of mind-body complementary medicine. Meditation offers an extreme state of relaxation and a serene mind.

During meditation, you concentrate your awareness and get rid of the flow of chaotic thoughts that may be cramming your mind and creating stress. This process may result in increased physical and emotional well-being. To shift into the meditation realm, however, we need to become involved with this object; we need to communicate with it. The result of this exchange, of course, is a deep awareness that there is no difference between us (as the subject) and that which we focus or meditate upon (the object). This leads us to the state of Samadhi, or self-realization.

For example, you might meditate on or think of a course of action regarding your child's education, or a career change that would involve a move across the country. Viewing a powerful movie or play, you may be moved to meditate upon the ethical issues plaguing today's civilization.

Although you don't need to formally meditate in order to practice yoga and the practice of yoga is not required in order to meditate, the two practices actually support one another. Through your practice of yoga, you've enhanced both your abilities to concentrate and to relax the two most important conditions for a meditation practice. Now you can deepen

your understanding of what meditation is and begin a practice
of your own.

Chapter Three
The Benefits of Meditation

The benefits of meditating are much publicized by those already undertaking daily or regular meditation. Deep physical and emotional changes take place when we meditate. This causes an actual shift in the brain and in the instinctive processes of the body.

Many have different reasons for desiring to meditate. No matter what your reason for wanting to meditate, it can be intimidating to know how to begin and how to continue to be encouraged. The health benefits meditation can produce naturally reflects on the mental and physical effects of this progress. You are meditating to let go of whatever you do not need.

Every day, more ways meditation will enrich your life are being realized. Here are several:

Improved Health

Meditation improves the immune system, so you will be more resistant to illnesses. In addition, the healthier routine will reduce the pointless pressure on your body. You may even save money on your medical expenses.

Better Creativeness

Are you creative? Even if you think you're not, you'll be amazed at how artistic you can be. You'll can learn any talent you've always wanted to develop, whether it to write a book, learn a new language (my husband is from Poland, I needed to learn) or play a musical instrument.

Better Reasoning Capabilities

Both your memory and ability to think will improve significantly. You'll feel much more alert. Imagine what this will do for your career.

Lowering Stress

You will find yourself more at peace. The Things that once made you anxious will no longer trouble you.

Better Relationships

Your thinking and behavior will be more loving and compassionate. You will also be able to listen better and use more caring way of speaking.

More Sense of Resolve

With greater clarity and development of your talents, you will find out how you can make a difference in the world. Helping other people is one of the most rewarding activities I have found. It will enrich your life in countless ways.

Greater Emotional Strength

Your feelings won't be hurt so easily, and people will no longer be able to push your buttons. Loneliness will be a thing of the past.

Chapter Four
Meditation Tools

Ultimately, we want to meditate to calm the mind, to relax the physical self, and to encourage an inner peace. One way to improve these exercises is by familiarizing yourself with spiritual tools into meditation rituals. Here are three tools that have been used since ancient times to assist individuals develop their meditative exercises.

Meditation cushions, also called zafus help to raise the body off the floor, so sitting for extended periods of time is made. The purpose of meditation cushions is to accommodate the body completely so the mind will be free to focus.

Mala beads are complicatedly knotted to the mental side of meditation. Each single bead on the chain represents an action or intention. The individual recites a mantra or some evocative phrase with every bead that's counted, constructing a rhythmic momentum while fully centering the mind in that particular present moment. The basic object of meditation malas is to foster determination behind every single step of your distinctive path.

Incense can represent the spiritual part of meditation. Burning incense represents the desire to burn away the superfluous layers of ourselves, exposing the true insubstantial quality within us. The flowing smoke at that moment represents our movement emerging onwards through the cosmos.

With these basic three, I'm going to add two things. Seiza bench, for people who are more at ease practicing on a meditation bench in the traditional Japanese kneeling posture, called seiza position. And, of course, a timer. With meditation, you can lose track of time easily.

Chapter Five
How to Meditate

After choosing a suitable environment where you won't be
interrupted for at least ten minutes or longer, sit down, relax
and rest your hands on your lap. If that's awkward or difficult
for you, then curl them in your lap or let them remain at your
sides. Whatever gives you the ability to free your mind and
focus on your breathing.

You can sit on the floor cross-legged with the assistance of a
bolster, or on any chair resting your feet on the ground. The
lotus position is not necessary if you are not used to it. No
matter how you sit, it is essential to maintain the natural
curve of your back. So, don't slouch. Individuals with
prolonged back difficulties who cannot sit for a prolonged
period of time can look into another meditation position.
When feel you're in a relaxed, at eased position and are ready
to get started, set your timer for the period of time you'd like
to meditate.

Tilt your head as though you're staring down helps open up the chest to relax your breathing. Breathe gently and deeply. Closing your eyes gently, train your soft, unfocused gaze downwards. You should inhale through your nose and exhale through your mouth when meditating. However, make certain your jaw muscles are relaxed, even though your mouth is somewhat closed. Don't grind your teeth; clench your jaw, etc. Just relax. Let it come to you and don't force your breathing. At first, your intake of air is going to be shallow. You will see as you allow more air to fill your lungs, your breaths will steadily become deeper and fuller. Take the time needed to breathe slowly and deeply.

Focus on your breathing. Instead of struggling not to think about the elements around you like that bill you forgot to pay or the traffic you'll have to fight; the situations that might stress you out, think about and concentrate on your breath. By directing all of your concentrating on your breaths, you'll notice that all other concerns from the outside world slip away on their own, without you having to fret about how to ignore them.

You will begin to feel calmer and more relaxed as you begin to breathe more deeply. This is a good indication. Begin concentrating your attention on your breathing. Be mindful of each breath that you take in through your nose and each breath that you exhale with your mouth. Continue focusing on your breathing for as long as you can.

If your attention begins to drift from your breaths, slowly bring it back. You may experience this many times. Don't give up. The most important thing to realize that you've strayed and you bring your focus back to where it belongs.

You can try counting your breaths if you're experiencing trouble refocusing your attention. You will soon see that as you improve your focus, you will find it easier to concentrate.

Some find it easier to keep their focus on inhalations than on exhalations. Keep this in mind if is what you experience. Put in the effort to concentrate especially on the feel of your breath as it exits your body.

Once again, don't beat yourself up. Admit that focus will be difficult for you when you're just beginning all beginners go through the inner chatter. Some would say that this recurrent return to the present moment is part of the training of meditation. What's more, don't expect your meditation practice to transform your life overnight. Mindfulness will take time before it will exert its influence. Keep coming back to meditate every day for at least a few minutes, lengthening your sessions when possible.

Now, stretch yourself and extend your increased consciousness and awareness to your daily activities.

Chapter Six
Five Different Ways to Meditate

Just as there are various styles of yoga, so there are many ways to meditate. The first phase of meditation is to focus on a distinct object or create a point of focus, with the eyes either opened or closed. You would silently repeat a phrase or word, audibly recite a prayer or mantra, visualize an image such as a deity, or concentrate on an item such as a lit candle in front of you. These are all commonly recommended points of focus. The perception or counting of your breaths and recognizing the bodily sensations are also optional focal points.

Sound

Chanting is a great way to enter into meditation. Longer than a mantra, chants include both cadence and notes. You can recite a prayer or affirmation which can be just as successful. Mantra Repetition is just a successful as chanting. The power of mantra is a great way to learn how to use sound for meditation. There are many mantras such as Om, Soham and

Guru Om. These mantras give a focal point for meditation, and over time, reinforce the mind, making it easy to focus. Music is another method of sound meditation is using music as a point of focus. There's a lot of music available out there. Some people find it very useful, helping them stay focused and awake during meditation. You may want to experiment with it and see if it works for you.

Imagery

Visualizing is also a good way to meditate; one that beginners often finds easy to practice. Traditionally, a meditator visualizes his or her chosen deity—a god or goddess-in vivid and detailed fashion. Essentially any object is valid. Some practitioners visualize a natural object such as a tree, the ocean, even a flower. Some meditate on the Chakras in the body. In this form of meditation, you focus on the area or organ of the body which corresponds to a specific chakra, visualizing the specific color connected with it.

Gazing

Another variation on the use of imagery is to maintain an open-eyed focus upon an object. Gazing meditation is the fastest, easiest meditation technique. The choices available to you are limitless. Candle gazing is a popular form of this method. But you can pick any object. Simply look at it without letting your eyes to interrupt contact. Yes, blinking is okay. Keep breathing. Focusing on a vase with a flower, a favorite statue, or a photo of a deity are added possibilities.

It requires no special postures or breathing techniques. There are no special mental exercises.

Breathing

Using your breath as a point of focus is yet another possibility. You can do this by essentially counting your breaths. Eventually, however, meditating on the breath just means purely observing the breath as it is, without changing it in any way. In this instance, the breath becomes the single objective of your meditation. You observe every degree of the breath and each impression it produces. For example, how it feels as it moves in and out of your nose, how it moves in your abdomen and chest, and so on. Though you are fully aware of all these details, you don't stay on them or criticize them in any way. You simply remain separate from what you're observing. What you find out is neither good nor bad; you merely let yourself to be with the breath from moment to moment.

Physical Sensations

Another way to meditate is to observe a physical awareness. You can use this with the equal amount of detail as you would when observing the breath. With this situation, you will look extremely at, or penetrate a specific sensation that draws your awareness, such as how hot or cool your arms feel. Observing a precise emotion or any specific area of discomfort is a possibility. Whatever you choose, continue as your point of focus for the whole practice. You possibly will find that examining a physical perception can be more challenging than observing the breath. For most beginners, mantras, chants, and visualizations offer more tangible ways to replace or calm the dispersed thoughts of our minds, which seems to be continually on physical overload.

Chapter Seven
Meditation Postures

Sitting

You can meditate, in any activity or position of serenity.
Sitting is the most generally suggested posture. There are a lot
of classic seated poses, but the Easy Cross-Legged Pose is
clearly the most basic. More lithe meditators prefer the Lotus
Pose.

Being seated in a chair similarly works. It's no less successful
and definitely no less spiritual. It's often the greatest option
for beginners. The most significant things are that your spine
remains upright and that you feel stable and comfortable. To
increase comfort on the floor, position a bolster or fold a
blanket under your behind to raise it and slightly direct your
knees down to the floor. This will help support the curve of
your lower back. Some individuals prefer kneeling. There are
small, slanted wooden benches you can buy for this pose.

Relax your arms then put your hands on your thighs or on
your lap and your palms facing up or down in a relaxed

position. Move your shoulders back. Next move them down then slightly raise the chest. Hold your neck long and your chin tilted somewhat downward. Depending on which style you are going by, the eyes might be opened or closed.

Reclining

Lying down is related to relaxation. Also used for this type of meditation is the classic Corpse Pose. On your back keeping your arms along your sides, you would lie down, with palms facing upward. Touch the sides of your heels together and allow your feet to drift away from one another, as you begin to become completely relaxed. Even though your eyes might be opened or closed, some individuals find it more stress-free to remain awake with their eyes staying open. A prone meditation is more physically restful than other positions. It requires a greater amount of awareness to stay awake and focused. Consequently, as a beginner, you may find it more challenging to meditate in this posture and not falling asleep.

Standing

Standing, another meditation practice can be very effective. As an alternative of sitting to meditate, standing can alleviate lower back pain and encourage a greater sense of internal stability. Stand in a straight, comfortable posture with your feet facing forward, approximately shoulder width apart. Your knees should be lax and your arms resting easily at your sides. Be sure to check if the whole body is aligned with good pose with your shoulders rolled back then down. Open your chest, with your neck long, head balanced on top, in addition to your chin parallel with the floor. Keep your eyes either opened or softly close them. As with any type of meditation, start with a short period of time.

Walking

A moving meditation may be a pleasant opportunity for you. The difficulty of this method is to walk calmly and deliberately, with every step developing into your focal point. Your destination, distance, and stride are all secondary. Relax your arms along your sides then move easily, synchronizing your breath with your footsteps. Or you can breathe with your pace. Two steps, inhale, two steps, exhale, or whatever you can manage. In this form of meditation, apply good posture; take deep breaths, as well as experiencing the motions of the body. The movement of your walking should be uninterrupted, so select a safe area with space to wander around, like a large field or park.

Chapter Eight
Meditation Tips

Posture

Most people worry about where to sit, how to sit, what cushion to use, etc. that's good and all, but it's not that significant to get your exercise underway. Don't get caught up in the how. Just do it. Start off by just sitting on a chair, on your bed or on a couch. If you're at all contented on the ground, then sit cross-legged. It's just for five minutes at first. You can worry Later about improving it so you'll be comfortable for longer period of time. It doesn't matter much in the beginning. Simply just sit somewhere quiet and comfortable.

To increase mindfulness, sit with a straight spine on the floor or in a chair. Imagine the top of the head touching the sky to maintain proper posture. Allow your eyes to remain open, but gaze downward to prevent environmental distractions if necessary.

Focus

A purpose of the meditation practice is helpful for staying focused. Common motivations include reducing stress or developing a more mindful outlook about life in general. Using a mantra related to the intention helps focus the meditation practice.

Notice the light, sounds, energy. Another focus is how the body feels. Sitting with your legs crossed is a common position for meditation, but some people don't feel comfortable this way. Experiment with different positions to help you find a comfortable meditation position that promotes focus.

Emotions

Get to recognize yourself. This routine isn't just about focusing your attention; it's about discovering in what manner your mind operates. What's going on inside there? It's ominous, but by looking, your mind stray, becomes frustrated, avoid unpleasant feelings

Check in with how you're feeling. As you first settle into your meditation period, simply try to figure out how you're feeling. How does your body feel? What is the state of your mind? See whatever you're drawing in to this meditation session as completely okay.

When you're finished, smile. Truly be thankful that you had this moment to yourself that you stayed with your commitment, which you showed yourself that you're dependable, where you took the chance to get to perceive yourself and make friends with yourself. That's an incredible two minutes of your life.

Thoughts

Your mind will stray. This is practically an absolute certainty. Simply, come back when you stray. There's no stumbling block with that. When you notice your mind wandering, just smile a little, and merely gently return to your breath. You might feel a little frustration, but it's perfectly okay to not stay focused, it's going to happen. This is the exercise, and you won't be good at it for a while.

Cultivate a loving attitude. When you become aware of thoughts and feelings that appear during meditation, and they will, look at them with a welcoming outlook. You might try staying with them a moment or two. See them as friends, not trespassers. Keep in mind, they are, in fact, a part of you.

Don't fret about clearing the mind. Don't worry very frequently that you're doing it wrong. Lots of individuals think meditation is about clearing your mind, or stopping all thoughts. It's actually not. This can occasionally develop, but it's not the objective of meditation.

We tend to need to avoid feelings like irritation, resentment, uncertainty; but an extraordinarily useful meditation practice has been to stay with the feeling for a while. You will fret that you're doing it wrong. That's OK, we all do. You're not doing it wrong. There's no precise manner to do it, just be delighted you're doing it.

Breaths

For beginners, maintaining focus during meditation is generally a struggle. Remaining mindful of sensations, thoughts, feelings, and even distractions help shift attention. Breathing is a main focus of meditation. Start off by taking long, deep breaths. Pay attention to how those breaths feel as they come in and out of the body is an approach to use throughout the meditation.

Place

The great thing about meditation is that you can perform it anywhere. You can do meditation as you walk someplace, in your office, when you're traveling or just sitting in a park. Sitting meditation is the exceptional place to start. You can even design an altar or a shrine that you can face when you sit in meditation, if that's what you prefer. Place on your altar a candle or items that mean something to you. You may even find items for your altar as you walk. Sometimes, they may even call to you.

Time

Recognize the value of your daily meditation and totally welcome it mentally and emotionally. Create a daily habit and remain patient as meditation grows stronger with repetition. Be accommodating with your time but make certain you have fifteen minutes every day. It is often easier for beginners who might become frustrated trying to focus for long periods of time to begin with a short meditation session. Meditating for no more than five minutes at a time works well in the beginning stages. Placing aside the small block of time each day helps the beginner make meditation a daily habit.

First thing each morning, do it. You may say you will meditate every day or later in the day, but then forget all about it. Leave yourself a note where you will see it in the morning as a reminder.

Really pledge yourself. Don't merely say, "Of course, I'll make an effort for a couple days." Actually make this a promise to yourself. In your mind, stay committed, for at least thirty.

Silence

Silence is excellent for meditation is healing. There is an abundance of meditation music around, but nothing beats simple silence. Sometimes, the sounds or music playing simply covers up the chitchat in your mind. When we sit in silence we essentially get to experience what our mind is doing.

Enjoy

Above all, it's necessary that you enjoy meditation. Don't expect meditation to constantly be easy or even peaceful. Meditation has really wonderful advantages, and you can get going now. Start off sitting just a little each day. Be considerate to yourself. There's only one of you.

Chapter Nine
Starting Your Own Meditation Practice

What do you wish to accomplish with your meditation? Many come to meditation for a broad range of reasons. Whether to create a spiritual connection, increasing their creativity, quieting their inner chatter, or to aid in visualizing a goal, don't over complicate your reasons. Meditation is just about relaxing and refusing to be caught up in the anxieties of everyday life.

Find a distraction-free area. Especially when you're just starting out, it's important to clear your environment of distracting sensations. Turn off the TV and radio, close your windows against the street noises outside, and close your door to noisy friends. If you share your home with roommates or family members, you may find it difficult to find a quiet space where you can focus on meditation. Ask the individuals you live with if they would be willing to keep quiet for the duration of your meditation exercise. Promise to come tell them as soon as you're finished, so they can resume their normal activities.

You can also employ the use of incense, a scented candle, a bunch of flowers, or can be great little touches to enhance your meditation experience. Dim or turn out the lights to help you focus.

To keep you from becoming sore, use a meditation cushion or even an old pillow or sofa cushion during long periods of cross-legged sitting. Since it does not have a back, it won't let you drop back and lose focus on your energy.

If you discover that sitting without a chair-back hurts your back, feel free to use a chair. Try to be present in your body and keep a straight back for as long as it feels comfortable, then lean back until you feel you can do it again.

You really do need to wear comfortable clothes. You don't want to wear restrictive clothing that might pull you out of your meditative thinking. Loose, breathable clothes like what you might wear to exercise or to sleep in, are frequently suggested.

Determine a time of day when you're relaxed. When you're more familiar with meditation, you might use it to settle you down at what time you're feeling anxious or overwhelmed. But if you're a beginner, you may find it tough to focus at first if you're not in the correct frame of mind.

Remove every diversion you can think of before you sit down to meditate. If you're feeling hungry, grab a light snack.

Be sure you have a timer in hand. You don't want to break your concentration by checking the time. You will want to make sure you practice your meditation for long enough. Use a timer for the duration of time you desire to meditate. Since your phone might have a built-in timer on it, you don't even need to purchase one. If it doesn't, you can locate many apps for your phone or computer that will time your periods for you.

I would say that you should have a time of daily meditation. The most significant thing is that you find a time that works best for you. Don't try to do too much too soon. You will be quick to get depressed and stop completely.

Chapter Ten
When and Where to Practice

To establish consistency, you should meditate every day at the same time also in the same spot. Decide on a place that is quiet, where you'll be undisturbed.

Usually, the morning is well thought out as the ideal time because you are less prone to be distracted by the strains of your day. Many individuals find that meditating in the morning helps them begin the day with a better degree of composure and self-confidence. On the other hand, if a morning schedule is an effort, try to mediate in the afternoon or early evening.

Posture

Choose a position that works comfortably for you. If you prefer sitting, whether it be on a chair or the floor, maintain an erect spine with your body relaxed. Keeping your the palms up or down, your hands should rest easily on your lap or thighs. If you decide on walking or standing, remember maintaining good posture is also critical, with your arms hanging freely by your sides. When lying down, place yourself in a symmetrical and comfortable position with the appropriate support under your head and knees if needed.

Method

Choose on your objective of focus. If sound interests you, build your own mantra, audibly or silently reciting a word or phrase specifically calming to you.

Affirmations also work. "I am completely healthy in mind, body and spirit" or "I love and approve of myself" as you breathe out. You can also use a recording of chants or listen to a relaxing piece of music.

If you decide on imagery, gaze upon an item placed in front of you like a candle, or a picture of your goal. You can also visualize your favorite spot with your eyes closed.

One way to observe your breath is to count it. Inhale for three to five counts and exhale for the same extent of time. Shift to merely observing your breath, notice the natural rhythm and the movement in your chest.

Any posture and method that you choose, stick with for the period of your meditation session. Once you discover whatever works for you, you may want to continue that practice indefinitely.

Chapter Eleven
How Do You Know If It's Working?

At first, you might feel uncomfortable meditating. Sitting for
five to ten minutes might bring about your legs cramp up or
to fall asleep, reclining poses may simply make you fall asleep,
or you may start feelings impatient or agitated by walking
slowly. On the other hand, you may have some insightful
occurrences the initial few instances you practice and then
straight days of trying to copy them. Don't worry. Meditation
should not bring about pressure or you feeling as if you are
physically hurting. If this happens, lessen the time spent on
your practice or change your position. If that doesn't work,
return to integrating a few minutes of meditation into your
practice.

If you still continue having concern with your meditation
routine, you may want to seek the direction of a skilled
teacher or the assistance of a group that meets on a regular
basis to meditate together.

Conclusion

The benefits of meditation are great with the ultimate goal for many being enlightenment. I would believe most individuals reading this does not have the goal of enlightenment in mind. However, the benefits of meditation consist of the physical, emotional and spiritual. Meditation can improve overall general health, concentration, and mental well-being. I have been meditating for 20 years now and cannot imagine how most individuals get through their everyday life without all the benefits of meditation.

With many benefits of meditation that one has to wonder why everyone isn't meditating. The best benefit of meditation it is 100% free, there are no gym membership fees to pay and only takes about ten to fifteen minutes per day. Another big benefit of meditation is there are no negative side effects. The advantages of meditation are numerous with no negative side effects, and it simply takes a little time per day. Maybe you should start meditating!

Frequently Asked Questions

How Long Do My Meditation Sessions Need To Be?

After you expand on your initial five minutes, try for ten to fifteen minutes a session since it seems to take about ten minutes or more for the mind to settle itself down.

How Often Should I Meditate?

You can meditate once a day. There are some people meditating in the morning and then again before they sleep. The choice is yours. Treat meditation as a routine that you'd do naturally every day.

Am I Betraying My Religious Beliefs When I Meditate?

Since meditation is associated with Eastern cultures and religions is why many people have mistakenly equated meditation with a particular religion when in essence, it is not. This is a myth. Meditation does not require you to believe in any deity; neither does it require you to give up your religious beliefs.

What Is The Best Meditation Technique For Beginners?

If you are just beginning meditation; starting with a meditation that will build up your concentration influence, such as the breathing meditation.

How Much Time I Should Set Aside To Meditate?

Ten minutes is a good start as you get used to meditating. Go at your own pace and try not to force yourself to do more than you're comfortable with.

Sometimes I Fall Asleep.

Lift your eyelids higher, keeping your gaze easy and unfocused, will keep the brain motivated and attentive. Allowing more light to enter the eyes is a good way to stay awake. When you are tired, it is much harder to concentrate, so you will have to put in more effort to stay awake. It is perfectly normal. Just keep trying.

Is The Difference Between Sleep And Meditation?

Sleep is what you do at night. It produces dreams. Meditation, is done while you are when you are awake. You will find, though, meditation can sometimes lead you to sleep when you allow your focus to continual wander.

It's So Hard to Concentrate.

Many people, including long-time meditators, have experienced occasions when they find their concentration is not as focused as they want it to be. So, it is important to be patient and compassionate with yourself, especially if you are a beginner.

My Mind Keeps Wandering While Meditating.

It will take time. Like mentioned above, it takes about ten minutes or more for the mind to settle itself down. Every time you meditate, you get that much better.

Who Shouldn't Learn Meditation On Their Own?

An individual who suffers from moderate to severe mental or learning incapacities should learn meditation under the supervision of an experienced trainer.

Is It Okay To Meditate After Eating?

Meditation is not waiting thirty minutes before you go in and swim, so you can meditate after eating. The brain is more to be expected to drift if you're hungry.

How Can I Ease The Chatter In My Mind?

See yourself in a white cube. There are no doors or windows. No up, no down, as you simply float. It should soon cease.

About The Author

Monique Joiner Siedlak is a writer, witch, and warrior on a mission to awaken people to their greatest potential through the power of storytelling infused with mysticism, modern paganism, and new age spirituality. At the young age of 12, she began rigorously studying the fascinating philosophy of Wicca. By the time she was 20, she was self-initiated into the craft, and hasn't looked back ever since. To this day, she has authored over 35 books pertaining to the magick and mysteries of life. Her most recent publication is book one of a Paranormal Urban series entitled "Jaeger Chronicles."

Originally from Long Island, New York, Monique is now a proud inhabitant of Northeast Florida; however, she considers herself to be a citizen of Mother Earth. When she doesn't have a book or pen in hand, she loves exploring new places and learning new things. And being the nature lover that she is, she considers herself to be an avid animal advocate.

To find out more about Monique Joiner Siedlak artistically, spiritually, and personally, feel free to visit her official website: http://www.mojosiedlak.com

Other Books by Monique Joiner Siedlak

Mojo's Wiccan Series

Wiccan Basics

Candle Magick

Wiccan Spells

Love Spells

Abundance Spells

Hoodoo

Herb Magick

Seven African Powers

Moon Magick

Cooking for the Orishas

Creating Your Own Spells

Mojo's Yoga Series

Yoga for Beginners

Yoga for Stress

Yoga for Back Pain

Yoga for Weight Loss

Yoga for Flexibility

Yoga for Advanced Beginners

Yoga for Fitness

Yoga for Runners

Yoga for Energy

Yoga for Your Sex Life

Yoga: To Beat Depression and Anxiety

Yoga for Menstruation

Beautiful You Series

Creating Your Own Body Butter

Creating Your Own Body Scrub

Creating Your Own Body Spray

Mojo's Self-Improvement Series

Manifesting With the Law of Attraction

Stress Management

Connect With Me!

I really appreciate you reading my book! Please leave a review and let me know your thoughts. Here are the social media locations you can find me at:

Like my Facebook Page: http://facebook.com/mojosiedlak

Follow me on Twitter: http://twitter.com/mojosiedlak

Follow me on Instagram: http://instagram.com/mojosiedlak

Follow me on Bookbub: http://bit.ly/2Kn1WOA

Subscribe to my YouTube Channel: http://bit.ly/2InCAQk

Made in the USA
San Bernardino, CA
29 June 2020

74393915R00035